Kitten Kindergarten

Kitten
Kindergarten

Practical help and advice
for your kitten's first year

MARIE TOSHACK

SMITHMARK

With thanks to my good friends, local veterinarians and pet behaviorists for their advice and experiences.

The publishers would like to thank Belinda Carpenter and Pets Paradise of Eastgardens Pagewood, Barbara Bikhazi and Strictly Pets of Newtown Sydney, and Tina Zollo and "Bronte" for their help and their kittens; and photographers Oliver Strewe and Ernie Kaltenbach.

This edition published in 1999 by SMITHMARK Publishers,
a division of U.S. Media Holdings, Inc.,
115 West 18th Street, New York, NY 10011.

SMITHMARK books are available for bulk purchase for sales promotion and premium use. For details write or call the manager of special sales, SMITHMARK Publishers, 115 West 18th Street, New York, NY 10011.

Produced by: Brewster Publishers Pty Ltd
PO Box 3231, Tamarama NSW 2026 Australia

ISBN: 0-7651-1029-6

Printed by South China Printing Co. (1988) Ltd, Hong Kong

10 9 8 7 6 5 4 3 2 1

Library of Congress Catalog Card Number: 98-61233

Contents

The primitive make up of the domesticated cat is all part of its feline attraction and charm. Throughout its life the cat is a free spirit and never allows the owner to overwhelm its personality.

There is always a feeling that the cat owns the human and, in many cases, the cat certainly chooses its owner by arriving at the door with cunning calculation.

Kittens cannot be trained like puppies but this does not mean they are stupid and cannot learn. Kittens always learn from watching what other cats do and best of all by watching their mothers. By the time a kitten is eight weeks old it will be quite independent.

Rewards—usually food—are the basis of kitten training, starting from answering its name and coming indoors. It is possible to train some kittens to press a button for a food reward. It is harder to make kittens unlearn their hunting instincts to stalk and destroy wildlife and birds. All kittens hunt and, if kept indoors, will hunt toys or even household objects.

Punishment or harsh discipline never works with kittens and cats, who will run away and hide or pack up and leave home.

This makes setting the house rules and training the kitten an important factor in its early life. Socializing, or kindergarten for the kitten, needs to take place in its first three months.

The ideal kitten is an indoor-loving, people oriented breed. Whether an old-fashioned reliable common mouser or pure bred, there is a huge variety of cats available to chose from. Look for placid breeds who love the quiet life; they will be more amenable to learning the rules of your kitten kindergarten than haughty self-centered and dominant cats.

Popular kittens

Abyssinian cats can be trained to perform tricks as well as train their owners to do exactly what they want. Abys have a lovely habit of using their paws to pick things up and often clutch their owners around the neck like a small child while keeping their claws sheathed.

Bengal cats will bathe, swim and drink from a running tap just like the Asian leopard cats in the wild. Prowls rather than walks and hunts toys rather than idly playing with them. Happy to walk on a leash, they are loving and outgoing.

British shorthairs have a penchant for lolling around the house all day. Intelligent, the British shorthairs make excellent pets that are easy to train—if not to keep on a diet.

British blues seem to share the phlegmatic British characteristics—placid with a gentle disposition.

Burmese cats are lively and affectionate natured cats. Real family cats that must have human interaction which makes them ideal inside pets. They are "talkers" like the Siamese but not as demanding.

Charteaux is an observer of life, not an aggressor. A quiet, tolerant breed. A good hunter but not a fighter.

Devon rex never just sits around looking elegant and bored—it always finds life amusing. Very easily cared for, the Devon rex is intelligent and resourceful.

Domestic shorthairs are the non-pedigreed moggies or mousers who make devoted and loving pets.

Egyptian maus have an effervescent and gregarious personality with a tendency to "chortle" to themselves.

Havana browns (named after the color of Cuban cigars) love to play hide and seek—leaping out from behind furniture to surprise (or frighten) people. Elegant and graceful, they can be very demanding, needing attention and praise.

Korats have a strong-willed, pushy nature. Gregariousness makes them playful and trainable, but they are set on always having their own way. More a one-person cat.

Ocicat is a gentle, playful and intelligent breed of cat. It responds well to early training but is not suited to prolonged solitude.

Oriental shorthairs are athletic and active. Orientals are shameless flirts who are very gregarious. They pine if they don't have human companionship and can become very bored.

Russian Blue is a quiet, sweet natured cat, making an affectionate, shy companion best suited to indoor living. It is devoted to its owners and the least destructive of cats.

Siamese are the chatty vocal cats. Strident in their talking and probably the most instantly recognizable of all breeds. Jealous by nature, they are immensely loyal to their owners. Lonely or ill Siamese become depressed; bored Siamese are destructive.

Tonkinese are less vociferous than their Burmese and Siamese relatives but have all the curiosity and affection of the Orientals. Intelligent and devoted companions rather than pets.

The Longhairs

Angoras are indoor cats which can occasionally enjoy a dip in the swimming pool.

Balinese are the kind of busy cats who are never happier than when underfoot and the center of attention. Inquisitive, they will thoroughly investigate cupboards and dive into shopping bags. Escape artists, they are almost able to pick locks to get outdoors.

Birmans can be demanding and bossy but they are very friendly cats.

Chinchilla and Persian cats have a fiery temper simmering underneath their appearance of aloof innocence. Temper tantrums can erupt when the long coats must be groomed every day. They also don't like being given medicine, hissing and striking their nearest and dearest is fairly common. Definitely dominant cats.

Himalayans are devoted to their owners, following them everywhere.

Maine Coons have amiable personalities and are happy to entertain themselves. A happy-go-lucky personality cat, with a chirping trill greeting to other cats and owners.

Norwegian Forest cats need exercise but cope well with indoor living. Highly intelligent and sociable.

Ragdolls have gentle natures, and are most suited to indoor living—easily trained with rewards and happily adapt to scratching posts—they take little interest in hunting.

When the kitten comes home

House rules for both owner and kitten should be set immediately after you bring the kitten home.

Kittens need an environment where they are liked and feel comfortable, even cosseted. They can understand voice tones—when you are angry, pleased or exasperated, and when you are praising them. They respond to their names and to being called. If they are hungry, they will run to the owner when called.

The rules

Set the house rules from the start. What a kitten does, it will do for life. Teach it to stay in at night and it won't yowl all through the house crying to be let out. Never answer a kitten meowing and clawing at the door during the night or you will be its servant for life.

Put on a collar with an identification tag as soon as it gets home, in case it wanders away and is found. Show it where to find the litter box, where it will eat and drink, and where it will sleep.

Establish a routine. Kittens are creatures of habit and a routine is essential. Otherwise you run the risk of a kitten waking you at all hours of the night demanding food; or crying to be let out; or leaping on the kitchen table when you are preparing a meal; or worse, jumping on the dining table when you are entertaining, as though this happens with every meal.

A kitten needs love when it is little as much as any domesticated pet. If it is treated like a piece of furniture it will never develop a personality that responds to people. This is the type of kitten that becomes aloof, never comes home except to eat, and attaches itself to friendly (or long-suffering) neighbors.

Sleeping arrangements

Kittens always choose a cozy place to sleep—which is 65 percent of the time—so providing a suitable bed or basket where you'd like them to sleep is important. Kittens prefer to sleep above ground level to see what is going on around them, which is a good hint for putting their bed on a shelf or chair (not too high for a new kitten or it may fall and break a limb).

A kitten, like a new baby, will cry the first few nights in a new home. It will miss its mother and siblings. A warm bed with a soft fleecy or furry cover, and a ticking clock (to mimic the mother's heart beat) or softly playing radio, will help it settle down for the night. Do not put its bed on a concrete or very cold floor in a laundry room or bathroom without a lot of warm old woolens or blankets.

Other pets

Never allow other resident cats (particularly tomcats) alone with the new kitten at night. After a few days, the resident cat can be allowed in for a minute or two under supervision to look at the sleeping kitten. Increase these exposures but leave nothing to chance to reduce the risk of fights or a territorial tom attacking (even killing) the kitten—or of one jealous adult cat running away from home in disgust.

If you have a dog, train it to accept the new kitten's presence. Plan its introduction carefully. Regardless of size, the dog will most likely be dominated by the kitten's hissing and a well-directed swot on the nose with a paw. Do not allow any dog unsupervised into the room where a new kitten is sleeping. When it is asleep, let the dog in to see and sniff it, then firmly take the dog out.

Even the best trained dog will occasionally chase a kitten belonging to the household.

Some dogs, it is said terriers especially, can be troublesome at initial contact.

Cozy corners

As the kitten grows, it will inevitably find inexplicable places around the house to sleep, such as sock drawers that have been left open, wardrobes and linen cupboards, small recesses behind or underneath sideboards or even in kitchen cupboards among the saucepans. If the kitten is missing, open and check all these unlikely places.

So be prepared; kittens tend to make up their minds where they are determined to sleep and have an iron will—even a veterinarian shamefacedly confesses his old cat prefers to crawl into his bed between the sheets on the coldest winter nights.

And if there is a new baby in the house, wisdom still advises to always keep the nursery door shut. Even older cats, not used to children, like to curl up in a cot next to the baby for its warmth. When little baby's hands reach out and pull the cat's ears and whiskers, scratches and accidents can happen.

Kitten litter

If this is your first kitten, litter is coming into your life. The shopping list will include a special "litter tray" (a rectangular plastic dish) and litter (a fine absorbent granule available at supermarkets). Make sure the sides of the tray are not too high for a small kitten to climb into. Powder or liquid deodorant is also used in the tray. Cover the bottom of the dish with litter and remove solids daily—an old pair of tongs or a plastic "poop scooper" are fine.

Some cat owners line the bottom of the box with newspaper, but it doesn't deodorize and the kitten's claws quickly shred the newspaper.

The litter should always be kept in the same place—show the kitten if you must move it somewhere else.

Always keep the litter away from small children and dogs. Pregnant women should never handle litter trays. A parasite, *toxoplasma gondii*, sometimes carried in the kitten's intestine, can be present in the litter and it is possible for the mother to pass it on to the unborn fetus. Pregnant women should also avoid touching garden soil in case a cat has used it as a toilet. Someone else can take over the gardening and litter emptying duties for nine months!

A kitten willingly selects litter over hard floors because it feels natural and allows it to cover or bury its droppings. Its mother will have already trained it to scratch its paws in sand.

One litter box for two cats is enough, but some cats will resent a new kitten using its box (a second litter is then essential). Cats also want privacy when using their litter box—keep it in a quiet, out-of-the-way place.

Kittens are fastidious and bitterly resent using dirty, wet litter. Keep it clean and change the litter when necessary (at least once a week). Tip the used litter into a strong plastic bag for disposal, then wash the tray with detergent and hot water, rinsing it with disinfectant or white vinegar. Make sure all stains and odors are removed before drying thoroughly and refilling.

Advanced house training

Some house kittens occasionally use the bath drain hole or even the laundry tub at times of feline emergencies when the litter box is dirty.

In space-limited New York apartments, some kittens have been trained to use the toilet bowl instead of a litter box. They also are curious about the toilet flushing, jumping up on the seat to look at the water. It is not too difficult to toilet train a kitten, once it is big enough to jump up and stand on the toilet seat, if you can't cope with the smell or inconvenience of a litter box in a small apartment.

Start by moving the kitten's litter box into the bathroom to get it used to the new location. Make a strong cardboard rim in the shape of a toilet seat, cover it with heavy duty plastic and then fasten it under the seat. Place just enough litter over the plastic to convince the kitten this is its usual tray. It will jump up and use it, learning to steady itself on the toilet seat. Long legged breeds are more agile at this maneuver.

The litter is then gradually reduced to half and holes are made in the plastic, allowing the urine to drip through. Within two or three days, the kitten should use the seat without the fake tray. The owner, who should preferably have a second

bathroom to use while the kitten gets used to its new routine, does the flushing.

Meals

Food blackmailing by cats starts young, so take a firm hand if the new kitten begins to refuse normal meals for whatever *you* are eating.

Kittens should be fed a little and often—at least three times a day with plenty of variety. Use dry or canned food, or fresh raw meat or chicken. The better canned foods are complete meals. There are good dried foods too (meat, chicken and fish flavors) which some kittens can become quite addicted to.

If you give raw meals one day, use canned foods the next. Dry food is a useful dietary supplement, but should be used with caution as it can cause serious urinary tract and kidney problems, particularly in male cats. Make sure dry food is less than ten percent of the kitten's diet and avoid the cheaper brands containing magnesium salts. Always check the label or buy only brands recommended and sold by veterinarians.

Raw meat, chicken, fresh rabbit and fish make tasty meals. Canned sardines in oil may appeal to some kittens and be ignored by others. Table scraps? Kittens do enjoy meaty left-overs, cheese and other bits and pieces.

Kittens and cats love eating fresh grass and you can buy special seed packets to grow sweet grasses in pots if the kitten is restricted indoors. This can also have the advantage of saving indoor plants from being chewed. When the kitten is ill, it will eat grass and vomit, however grass is normally part of a kitten's diet.

Kittens should always be fed in one place and quickly learn if they will be fed when they come inside at night. If you have more than one kitten, it is sensible to feed them separately in the same room to stop them from eating their food too quickly and to make sure the smaller, shyer one gets its fair share.

Always keep a clean dish of fresh water (changed daily) beside the food dish. If a kitten drinks excessively, it needs veterinary attention.

Calling kittens home

A kitten quickly learns its new name, no matter how inappropriate it may be, and responds to it when called. Successful training involves conditioning the kitten (using food treats is the best way) to respond to your command. These early training sessions to come should never be more than a couple of minutes.

Initially the kitten is rewarded every time it performs the command—coming forward as you say its name and the word "come." Through trial and error find a treat that your kitten craves, something already in its diet or even the flavors of yeast-based vitamin tablets. Begin by feeding the treats by hand, then raise your hand above the kitten's head so it must rise up on its hind feet to get the treat.

Once the kitten has adapted to the treat, show it the treat in your hand, then step back and say, "Come," as the kitten moves toward you. Increase the distance until the kitten will come from another room.

When the kitten understands what it must do to earn its reward, switch to other associations such as banging a can of cat food with a spoon when you call the kitten, then giving it some as a treat. Shaking a packet of dried food also attracts the kitten.

The food treat can be phased out once the kitten responds to the associated sound. A "clicker" or whistle is also used as an association by professional trainers, which is less intrusive than repeatedly calling out the kitten's name from the back door.

Training your kitten to come when called is vital to attracting an outdoor kitten inside when you are going out. But kittens will ignore calls to come home if they are sleepy or stalking—or simply feeling unsocial. If you can see the kitten, go and pick it up, carry it indoors with lots of cuddling, and give it a treat. It is a good idea to train your kitten to meow when it hears its name called, even when it is hiding.

Do not call a kitten only to give it punishment or medicine; that never leaves a good association.

Cat flaps

To avoid being used for the rest of your feline-owning life as a "kitten butler," install a cat flap in a door, window pane or even a hole made in a wall for the kitten to come and go as it pleases. The flap can be secured at night to keep the kitten indoors, which is now law in many towns and cities. Remember to make the flap big enough for when the kitten is fully grown.

Commercial flaps (usually plastic) have two swinging see-through flaps, one outward and one inward. The locks are designed to allow you to stop the kitten going either in or out, but many kittens quickly learn how to claw open the small catches and the flaps. Even large weights or boxes placed in front of the flap can be pushed out of the way by clever kittens wishing to make an escape.

It is 100 percent safer to use a flap than leave open a window. However, make sure the flap is placed far enough from the door and window bolts to prevent long-armed burglars reaching through.

Cat flaps can cause problems. The home is the kitten's sanctuary, the place where there is no threat of attack or competition, a place where interlopers are excluded. Once you install the cat flap, it does allow other cats, not just your kitten, to enter the house at will. It allows them to eat your kitten's food and do anything they like. The feline social order is disrupted. As a result, the rightful house kitten may show signs of stress by becoming timid, or it may begin urinating and defecating inside the house, while the stray cats will also spray inside the house to establish it as their new territory. Also, there may be noisy cat fights.

To keep out other cats, switch to electronically locked models and activators attached to the kitten's collar. Only kittens wearing the special collar can open the door which locks firmly behind them.

Training kittens (and grown cats) to use the new cat flap is easy. Wedge or tie open the flap until the kitten gets used to the opening. Gradually, you can lower the flap and call the kitten, using the lure of food just inside the flap. Most kittens pick this up quickly or try giving the kitten a gentle push through the flap.

Other cheaper homemade cat flap systems use a hidden access hole somewhere in the house to allow the kitten to come and go more or less secretly—hopefully out of sight of dogs or marauding stray cats.

In a kitten's world

Modular "adventure" playgrounds with long cages, tunnels, walkways, sleeping platforms, climbing towers and exercise runs can be installed outdoors around shrubs and lawns, but still connected to the house through a cat flap.

These modules keep the kitten safely confined while playing or sleeping outside in the yard, provide exercise and stimulation during the day or night and safe access back indoors. While the kitten is happy to be outdoors, it is restricted from hunting wildlife or wandering onto busy roads. It is also dog-proof.

If the owner must go away for short periods, the system also allows the kitten to stay in its normal safe environment, with someone coming in to give it fresh food and water every day.

Kittens like:

- elevated perches such as a roof (where the sun can be followed throughout the day);

- safe spots under trees and shrubs for snoozing;

- a small part of the garden with sand or loose soil as a private kitten toilet area;

- bushy or overgrown areas where they can hide;

- well-branched trees for scratching and climbing;

- dog-proof fences;

- easy access to their cat-flap.

If all these are available, kittens are more likely to stay around their own yards and keep out of trouble.

Learning to lead

As it grows the kitten will love to walk around the garden with the owner, but once it ventures outside the front fence, a light (puppy) leash attached to its collar will keep it from running away or onto a busy road if frightened.

Use the leash inside the house to start with, then, once the cat is used to being restricted, go for short walks outside.

Walks will be slow and very much at the kitten's pace. It will stop, sniff, maybe run a little bit, then lie down. It will want to make all the detours around the yard that kittens normally do alone. Cats mark their territory (scratching and urinating) just like dogs and check out if other cats have passed that way. There will be favorite patches of sweet grass to chew, spots of loose dirt to roll in and mice to chase.

Much patience is required, rather like walking a dog who sniffs every post or tree in a park. Let the kitten take its time if it must be confined indoors 99 percent of the time. Evening walks along a footpath will be quicker once the kitten is accustomed to this strange human restraint and pace of traveling.

Games and tricks

Cats' natural feline actions—just watch a cat leap from fence top onto a roof—can be used for trick jumping. Crouch behind your kitten, bringing your arms together in front of it. Get it used to walking over your hands, then by placing your hands higher, get it to jump over.

Kittens will not always do tricks such as rolling over or meowing on command. Instead they may simply walk away in disgust if they are not in a playful mood.

Kittens are very playful and love chasing anything that moves:

- crumpled bits of paper;

- small sheets of newspaper twisted and tied with a string and pulled away from the kitten;

- small plastic balls (the kind used for Christmas tree decorations) or ping-pong balls;

- small round nuts which roll noisily across the floor and ricochet loudly off the walls;

- a long ribbon, twine or string, or anything tied onto elastic.

Keep on the lookout for these kitten toys:

- catnip stuffed toy mice;

- soft balls with bells;

- wind-up toy mice;

- rubber rats;

- high-tech toys such as toy mice that move when activated by a kitten's paw.

Most owners get tired of these games before the kitten ever does. But even older cats that find plenty of mental stimulation outdoors chasing mice or patrolling their territory, can suddenly start playfully chasing their tail, leaping in and out of boxes or pouncing on toys.

If toys and playthings are always available, the kitten is less likely to suddenly jump out, clawing and biting ankles or pounce on precious objects around the home.

House manners

Have kittens turned furniture scratching into an art form—could that sadly ripped chair or upholstered sofa be a form of "cat painting" as one theory of feline aesthetics (*Why Cats Paint* by Heather Busch and Burton Silver) claims? If so, nearly all cat owners possess masterpiece originals from those sharp little claws.

All kittens scratch by instinct—to sharpen their claws and stretch their muscles. Sadly, it also marks their territory indoors by leaving visible claw marks, rips and holes in various precious things. Notice, if you have more than one cat, how one will usually scratch a particular chair while another will have its own favorite activity like trying to run up and tear the curtains.

Vertical blinds are a definite no-no with cats in the house.

Try providing scratching posts—a good thick branch sawed for firewood, placed on a plastic flower pot saucer to catch the bits of bark. Alternatively, try a solid wooden box covered with carpet. Place it in a prominent place where the kitten can use it undisturbed.

Introduce the kitten to the scratching post or carpet box as soon as it can walk—before it can get used to your furnishings. Once the kitten is using the scratching post and ripping the carpet covering to shreds, you can move it gradually, day by day, until it is in a more convenient place.

Some owners resort to having the sharp ends of the claws trimmed but this leaves the kitten at a dangerous disadvantage, unable to climb trees to escape from dogs. De-clawing is a surgical method which leaves the kitten totally defenseless and is frowned on by animal lovers.

Anti-social behavior

Cordial neighbor relationships can be easily disrupted by kittens; they are never ideal conciliators. Kittens leap over fences without regard to legal niceties of ownership, spray the neighbor's yard, dig up plants, hunt and kill bird life. Cats fight at night—loud ear-splitting, pitched battles and yowling—waking the whole neighborhood at 2 a.m.

Put a small area of sand in a quiet corner of the yard. Encourage the kitten to use only that—and not neighbors' yards—as an outdoor toilet. Scratch its paws in the surface, the way you introduced it to the kitten litter box, from the time it first goes outside. If you see the kitten digging in the garden beds, pick it up and take it back to the special kitten toilet area.

All male kittens should be neutered at six or seven months of age to discourage straying, spraying and fighting. Use a strong pressure hose to wash away that unmistakable odorous spraying by stray tom cats. Then apply a liberal solution of water and white vinegar as a deodorizer to stop every other cat (including your own) from marking the same area. Never encourage stray cats by feeding them or they will move in on both you and the neighbors for life—with all their bad habits.

Kittens should be always locked in at night and not let out until they have used their litter trays in the morning. If complaints are still made about your kitten digging carefully tended flower beds, keep it indoors and hope this breaks the habit.

Save the birds

Attach bells and reflective tape to the kitten's collar if it is allegedly seen hunting or killing birds. Flashes of light from the tape and noise from the bells as it jumps may alarm birds in time to fly away. Try confining the kitten indoors until at least 8 a.m. or 9 a.m. when birds have finished their early-morning feeding.

Try not to allow the kitten to eat or play with dead birds and bury them.

Do not throw breadcrumbs or seed on the ground to attract birds. Even a bird feeder suspended from a high tree does not always work—birds that are messy eaters spill the seed, then fly down to eat it off the ground, offering a tempting target to any cat.

If you plant thick, bird-attracting shrubs, prune the lower branches that put the birds in a perilous position when feeding too close to the ground.

It is the law of the jungle out there.

Aggressive kittens

Scrapping and brawling around the neighborhood, with battle scars and torn ears—this is not the life for your innocent new kitten. Start socializing it early, playing with it and handling it. Sit it on your lap and stroke it quietly while you are watching television.

Get it used to being patted on the back (dominating) before you stroke it under the chin and chest (less dominating). This prevents the kitten growing up into a touchy, grouchy cat that bites and hisses every time it is touched, even by its long-suffering owners. Brush and comb the coat every day to get it used to being touched all over, especially if it is long-haired. Encourage it to socialize with other kittens.

Chastise it firmly if it chases visiting cats. Be firm, bring your kitten inside and do not immediately reward and praise it for fighting. It may only have been defending its territory, but this is the path to wounds, scars and abscesses.

Kittens behaving badly

There are strong-minded kittens who are convinced they are the "top cat," not the owner. This is not simply a misunderstanding. The owner must establish who is the boss when the new kitten first comes home.

Never let the kitten boss you. It is not a game if the kitten pounces at you and bites your ankle—it will be a more serious assault when it is fully grown, with sharp claws and

fangs and a bad temper. Raise your voice, clap your hands and shoo the kitten away and it will soon know you will not tolerate such naughty behavior, not even as a game. Get its toys out.

No kitten enjoys being grabbed and having medicine pushed down its throat, but be firm, be strong about it, and make sure the kitten swallows its dose. Sometimes a wily, recalcitrant cat will appear to swallow the medicine, then produce frothy yellow drool from its mouth 10 minutes later from a melted, wasted pill.

Watch the veterinarian administering pills. Try laying the kitten down on a towel on a table and roll the towel up quickly and firmly until the kitten is cocooned from the neck down—which stops it kicking and clawing viciously at your hands.

Hold the bundle firmly, push the jaws open and put the pill down the back of the throat with the index finger, then close the jaws and rub the throat until it swallows. As the animal grows and gets used to regular pill taking, it will accept it with better grace. Vicious clawing and biting must never be tolerated. Some kittens will chew up pills and swallow them when put in front of them, but these are, alas, few and far between.

Ear drops, which kittens bitterly hate, are best applied after rolling the cat in the towel, applying the drops, then rubbing the ear as directed by the veterinarian.

Long haired kittens that are not combed, particularly in the molting season, develop thick, matted knots in their fur. If these are not cut out immediately, it can result in one vast matted area causing the poor animal intense pain as the skin is pulled. Eventually the coat will have to be shaved under general anesthetic by a veterinarian. The kitten comes home in a sore and sorry state, through no fault of its own.

Often it is just a matter of finding a suitable wider plastic comb and softer brush which doesn't hurt its sensitive skin, to get the kitten used to a daily grooming.

Using the new-generation flea drops every five to six weeks instead of old-fashioned heavy flea powder, which seemed to make the long fine fur more static and liable to instantly knot, has made daily combing easier for both owner and kitten, without elbow-to-fingertip scratches and bites—and stretched tempers all around.

Psychosomatic kittens

Stress-induced anxiety causing various behavioral problems can mask itself as chronic medical conditions such as itchy skin, vomiting and bladder infections among highly-strung kittens.

Acupuncture by veterinary practitioners has been successful in treating these behavioral and emotional problems—but it may also be up to the owner to reduce stress in the household if it is so upsetting the kitten. Owners are usually compassionate and more than willing to invest the necessary time and management in treating the kitten, giving it love and attention. Veterinarian consultation may help with medication.

Wool eaters

Kittens who have been abandoned or found orphaned before they have completed the normal suckling period may pathetically suck a rug or blanket, rather like the Peanuts character Linus sucking his thumb and hanging onto a grubby old bit of a security blanket. They may suddenly start pummeling soft cushions, "kneading" with their paws, or even trying to suck at its owner's fingers. Owners should display patience—kittens settle down when mature and outgrow this behavior, with only occasional mental regressions into their sad kittenhood.

Some breeds (usually strains of Siamese) indulge in wool-eating, known as pica. Restricted to specific genetic lines, this very odd activity seems to be an inherited, ingrained trait. It begins in adulthood in cats weaned normally, rather than continuing from kittenhood in individuals weaned too early.

It is hard to live with a wool-eating kitten. Once it is relaxed, its eyes glaze, its paws knead and it licks at the nearest woolen object. The kitten tugs at the wool, sucking and chewing simultaneously. Some kittens only go this far, others chew and swallow large amounts of wool. (It could even be where all those missing odd socks disappeared to!) They also suck and chew human hair.

If the kitten begins vomiting up bits of wool or appears sick and constipated, it may need a dose of special laxative or oil, or a veterinary consultation. Wool eaters never seem to grow out of this habit.

Some kittens may start chewing rubber and electrical cables. Others take a liking to indoor plants or will rush to the shopping bags and start chewing the celery. There is no accounting for kittens' tastes.

Jealous cats

Introducing a new human baby or new kitten to the household can cause quite severe behavioral problems in the incumbent cat. There are common anti-social ways of showing its severe displeasure—urinating in strange places such as beds or on top of the stove. Some cats will refuse to eat; knick-knacks can be knocked off shelves; others will start to destroy every soft furnishing in the house. Occasionally the disturbed cat will begin to wash itself excessively by licking at paws, flanks and tail until the area is raw and bleeding.

The seriously unhappy cat, which regards itself now as unloved and displaced by this "intruder," needs constant cuddles and reassurance. Find time to re-introduce the old toys it enjoyed playing with as a kitten, particularly pulling a long string for it to chase. Nurse it, patting and talking to it. Do not leave it alone in a room with the baby, but do not rush at it, smacking or shooing it away when it goes near the nursery. Pick the cat up, pat it and carry it to another room, giving it a few treats to eat.

Introduce kittens carefully to incumbent cats—house the kitten, with its own litter box, food and water, and warm bed in a separate room until the older cat gets used to it and its smell in the home. Gradually move the kitten and its paraphernalia to establish its right of presence throughout the house. Even pour some of the damp litter from its box into the cat's big box. Begin feeding them alongside each other, standing close by to supervise. The kitten, used to its mother and siblings, will be unafraid of the resident cat sniffing it.

A kitten in your life

If a kitten is chased outside it may run up to the top of a tree and not be able to get back down. Plaintive cries can be heard but the kitten refuses—or may be too frightened—to move. If it is a particularly high and smooth-barked tree, the long-suffering fire department with its extension ladders may come to the rescue. But it is usually a case of waiting for the kitten to find the courage to back down to the nearest branch, hanging on to the trunk with its claws, coming down backwards until it is close enough to jump down to the ground.

Kittens can be stranded up to 48 hours before getting hungry enough to find their way back to ground level.

Traveling kittens

If taking your kitten on trips, or even just to the veterinary clinic, buying a cat carrier is a wise long-term investment. A wild-eyed kitten breaking out of a flimsy cardboard box on a freeway and leaping onto the driver's chest is not an experience most owners ever want to repeat.

Carriers are available from veterinarians and pet stores in either solid plastic, or wire and plastic, or fabric mesh. The old wicker carriers are attractive to the kitten because they obstruct its view (kittens don't like seeing movement and large loud shapes looming so close to the car) but are hard to clean when soiled. Line the bottom of the carrier with an old towel or newspaper which can be discarded along the way, and always carry plenty of replacements. Emergencies do happen.

Get the kitten used to the travel carrier by leaving it open on the floor at home, placing some of its toys inside and letting it play and sleep inside until it feels this is a part of its territory.

If you use it only to take the kitten to the veterinarian, it will quickly disappear outside or under the bed when it sees the carrier.

Lock the kitten in a room where it can easily be caught. Be firm and very fast when you put the kitten in the carrier, quickly pushing down the lid and locking it. Kittens fight fiercely, with the strength of dogs, if they hate traveling.

Once it is in the carrier, do not be tempted to let it out in the car during the journey. It can make a sudden leap for freedom out of a partly-open window or hide under a seat.

Have a collar and lead firmly attached if you must take the kitten out of the car on family comfort stops. Dogs or passing cars can terrify kittens, who might suddenly race into bushes beside the roadway never to be seen again.

Be prepared for the loudest crescendo of yowling protests once the journey is under way. Kittens wail endlessly, loudly and piti-fully, usually until you are well out of the city where the passing heavy traffic seems to terrify them.

After some time, the kitten's voice becomes hoarse and it gradually settles down to sleep

or watch proceedings with a beady eye from the cat carrier. Try to place the carrier where the kitten can always see the owner and speak often and consolingly to it.

In hot weather, make sure the kitten is not overheated and panting. Keep the car cool. If the kitten appears distressed (heat stroke), offer it water and wipe it with a wet washer.

Kittens on vacation

Once you arrive at your destination and let the kitten out of the carrier, it will probably disappear in a flash to investigate its new environment. It may well ignore your calls until the next day. Let it out without a meal and leave a door or window open (provid-ing it is a peaceful and remote area) and the kitten will usually come inside during the night when all is quiet. It will always be back for food when it gets hungry.

Keep the kitten indoors (with a litter tray) if it is a strange or crowded locality, until it gets used to the surroundings. Most kittens will sleep very soundly after the strain of a car trip, then be up exploring happily the next day.

City kittens enjoy the country where they find many interesting strange smells of the wild and a much quieter environment than they are used to at home. Sheds, wood heaps, orchards, rabbits and overgrown country gardens are a big attraction for city kittens.

Be prepared to lock the kitten up when you start to pack to return home—it may hide in order to prolong the joys of a country vacation.

The kitten may again be unsettled on the return trip, but do not worry. A kitten that does not take kindly to cars nor appears to enjoy traveling, often has a great time once it has arrived. It may be easier finding a live-in kitten-sitter or boarding facility while you go on vacation, but it may be a lot less stimulating for your kitten.

Moving house

Make sure the kitten is secured in one room on moving day, until you are ready to leave the old home, because with all the noise of packing and cleaning, its alarm antennae will be on full alert.

When you arrive at the new house, keep the kitten in a room with an emergency supply of litter and a dish of water while you make sure all the windows and doors are closed. Then let it out to thoroughly explore its new territory. Once the familiar furniture and the kitten's bedding from the old house are unpacked, it will feel more secure. Keep the kitten in the house for a few days until it settles down. When it starts snoozing on sofas again, that is the sign the kitten is relaxed. Then go outside with it for short periods until it learns its way around.

When the kitten first goes outside alone, make sure it has an empty stomach to encourage it back soon for food. Leave a door open in case of emergency—the kitten may need a quick escape from strange cats it encounters in the new garden.

If it is very frightened by its new surroundings the kitten may not want to leave the house for some time. Alternatively, the kitten may stay out very late or even until the following night, when all is quiet and it can make its way back to its new home. Go outside when it is dark or just before dawn and call it quietly. It may be hiding under a shed or nearby house until it feels secure enough to come back out.

Some kittens may even try to find their way back to their old home (un-neutered toms are the more likely). If this happens, and the kitten is found, it should be kept indoors for at least a month until the new house becomes the center of its territory and the source of food and shelter. Once kittens know you are staying, they will only rarely leave.

Can your kitten talk?

Well, yes—if you know how to translate, that is. You can call in a specialist "cat whisperer" to communicate with the "inner kitten" the same as the mysterious horse whisperers "talk" to horses, Robert Redford style. This may not be whispering so much as exchanging long, analytical looks at the kitten so it can express its desires, dislikes and problems, psychic-style.

Psychic-like, cat whisperers receive "messages" straight from the feline minds, first as flashes, then these turn into simple words and phrases—like clairvoyants.

Cat whisperers (who are also receptive to other animals, including racehorses) may not be for every misunderstood and underrated suburban kitten on the block, that secretly yearns for more understanding and consideration from its stress-ridden, career-driven owners.

However, alternative practices for animals are growing. In fact, there are Holistic Veterinary Associations that support "cat whispering" as a barely understood gift that can be developed into a skill, part of the growing ideas of the relationship between

human and animal. There are also animal spirit channelers (to find answers in earlier lives) and animal hypnotists. Kittens and cats of the future have much to look forward to as owners are only beginning to guess what the "inner kitten" is really thinking and saying.

Learned academic cat behaviorists have long studied and explored the interpretation of basic kitten talk, if not their innermost dreams, past lives, spirit guides and fantasies. They have uncovered distinctive kitten murmurs (with mouth closed), kitten calls (with mouth open then slowly closing while the sound continues), and kitten cries (with a tense mouth that stays open throughout).

And no matter where kittens live or what their living standards are the essential cat language remains the same; they express themselves in a similar fashion around the world.

Kitten conversation

Interpreting this language will assist with kitten training when the owner can communicate at the kitten's level:

- Purring:
  Always assumed to be the obvious non-hostile sign of a happy, contented kitten. Rough purring is an expression of intense pleasure.

- Smooth purring:
  Less loud and with no individual beats. It indicates the kitten has had enough of whatever pleased it and is about to stop.

- Loud smooth high purr:
  Designed to attract the owner's attention (listen for the "rrr" sound). Could it be there is something the kitten wants—food, for instance, or to sit on your lap and whisper secrets?

- Distress purring:
  The kitten is calling attention to its need for urgent help. It may be sick or in pain. Unobservant owners can miss this signal.

- Kitten murmurs:
  The greeting murmur, a kitten "hello," which is similar to the "smooth purr," but is, in fact, a "mrrr." If it is excited, it may express it as a trilled "rrr" sound.

- Calling murmur:
  Sounds like an "uh" noise to start with and means the kitten wants someone to "come here." It varies from a gentle plea to a sharp demand. This is often heard at the door.

- Acknowledgement murmur:

  A sort of "mhhng" sound, when the kitten is hoping to be given a special treat.

- Coaxing murmur:

  More insistent, a "mrrraahou" demand. "Do as I tell you."

- Drawn-out "meow":

  A call familiar to all kitten owners. "Feed me!"

- Begging call:

  A variation of the demanding call, a "mhrhrhrnnaaaahooouuu" drawn out as the mouth slowly closes. "Please won't you let me have that?"

- Bewildered call:

  Louder and more drawn out than the rest of the meow. A "maahouuuu" tells you the kitten is pretty darned excited about something. "What is going on here?"

- Worried call:

  A "maaouuuu" with twitchy body language expressing the kitten's concern. "Am I being ignored?"

- If you ignore the kitten long enough call:

  A "mhhngaahou" will plainly show displeasure. "Why are you doing this to me?" If the call fades away weakly the kitten is plainly saying, "And you said I was your best friend," and it is time to pick up the kitten for a big cuddle or the tidbit of food it may have expected.

- Yowling:

  Cries that are not among mankind's favorite sounds because they are a good indication of cat fights. The scream of a cat is more a screech than a scream, according to its intensity. "I am in pain, watch out!"

- Refusal cry:

  Low-pitched and raspy "oe-oe-oe-oe" when the kitten is standing its ground—"Get off!"—or taken by surprise.

- Spitting & hissing:

  Spitting ("Pffft") and hissing ("hssss") at humans or other cats means something unpleasant is about to happen. The more ominous "chchchchchchchch" spitting at other cats is a crude warning. "Back off!" Often a scuffle or fight can be avoided by prudent spitting at the opponent.

- Anger wail:

  An eerie, out-of-body noise which cuts through the night usually when two cats are only standing-off, not even in mortal combat. The cat's mouth opens and emits a long drawn out sound, "wwwaaahoooouuww," showing off its fangs to their fearsome best advantage by tilting back its head. "Don't come any closer or I'll bite!"

Usually the cat is happy if the owner appears to chase the other cat. It may even set off in mock pursuit, but secretly it is happier to go back indoors. The owner has, in the cat's view, actually supported it in the victorious fray.

- Growling, snarling, gurgling, wailing and howling:
  When cats fight.

- Hunting noises:
  Sounds like strange little "clicks" in irregular bursts that occur as the kitten stalks prey. A definite, "I'm going to sink my fangs right into you." If an indoor kitten spies a bird outside a window and cannot stalk and pounce, its teeth may chatter; it will open and close its mouth, softly making odd teeth gnashing "chutterchutter" noises. "Watch out, I'm coming after you."

- People attracting calls:
  All kittens resort to these in emergencies—little squeaks and almost inaudible plaintive cries. Always respond without delay—even in the middle of the night. It may mean the kitten is badly injured if it has access to outdoors.

- Chirruping:
  A mother cat gives a soft little "chirruping" noise when she wants her kittens to come to her or to follow her. Adult cats will use the same signal greeting their human owners, treating the humans as their kittens rather than as their mothers. "Come along, come with me." They will also make this sound when they bring home dead prey—quickly pry the kitten's jaws apart to remove it.

Body language

Kittens make themselves perfectly clear with their body language. Decode those tails:

- Tail raised slightly and curved softly means the kitten is interested in something;

- Tail lowered and fluffed out indicates the kitten is afraid;

- Tail held straight out and fully bristled—the kitten is in aggressive mode;

- Tail curved gently down and then up again at the tip reveals a happy relaxed kitten who has no worries;

- Tail lowered and tucked up under the body is a signal that the kitten is stressed or has been defeated;

- Tail straight up in the air means a welcome greeting (carried over from kittenhood when the kitten would present itself to the mother cat for inspection);

- Twitching tail signals the kitten is alert;

- Tail held still with the tip twitching means the kitten is mildly irritated;

- Tail swishing angrily from side to side usually means the kitten is about to attack;

- Tail held erect and quivering can be mistaken for urine-spraying, but is usually a reaction to friendly greeting by owner;

- Kittens who flatten their ears mean trouble, they are annoyed. Twitching their ears is another sign of anxiety.

The Kitty Café

The
Kitty
Café

Healthy, easy to prepare,
homemade food for
your cat

MARIE TOSHACK

SMITHMARK

With thanks to all the good friends who delved into their favorite home made recipe collections, particularly Pat Fleet, Kath Wilson, Helen Rook and their families of animals. And to "Golly Gosh," "HG," "Roy" and "Grumps," the cats in my life, who happily tested the recipes.

Sincere thanks for the generous and freely given time and expert help from Dr Arthur Poynting, of the Gloucester Veterinary Hospital, and the staff of the Gladesville Animal Hospital, Sydney, in particular Dr. Max Zuber and Dr. Pam Short.

The publishers would like to thank Terry Goulden and Spotted Mist "Peach," Christine Kindred and British Shorthairs "Spooky and Kucinta," Lorrie Philips and Cornish Rex "Silverwhite," Jon Sternbeck and Scottish Fold "Ptah Tinkerbell," Tina Zollo and Himalayan Persian "Bronte," Gauja Cattery and Balinese "Chanda, Blueberry and Strawberry," Gary Kurzer and Virginia Aghan and Birman "Henry," Judy Sibilia and "Kanishka." Also thanks to Megan Guest, Cat Control, Royal Agricultural Society of New South Wales, Seaforth Veterinary Hospital, Oliver Strewe and Ernie Kaltenbach.

Contents

D O YOU want a cat? Do you really need a cat? Cats don't always have to be bought; many of us have cats pushed at us. Cats will decide just who they will move in with and many a cat has arrived in the middle of the night with a pitiful meow. One morning you might find that a stray cat has had kittens under your oak tree or she might bring them by the scruff of the neck, one by one, across a busy road to find that smorgasbord you always put out for her.

Ours has always been a house cats are attracted to, as though there is some secret sign ("a soft touch here" in invisible cat writing?) on the front path. We have four—and I am allergic to (some, not all) cats.

How much will it cost to keep a cat in the style it will soon become accustomed to? Domestic mousers eat around the same as aristocats (pedigreed cats) but, like the poem "The Grandmother's Cat", some cats can eat a whole lot more. There are all kinds of cats— short-haired, long-haired, alley cats, show cats, dull cats, plain smelly cats, pushy and greedy cats, aloof cats-who-walk-by-themselves, sweet and affectionate cats.

Select-a-cat
Long-hairs with class

Angora
Long-haired Turkish breed with oriental-type body, and a medium to long Persian-type coat. Sheds (just as Angora woolens do) and grooming is required.

Balinese
Rare long-haired Siamese, with a dark, plumed tail and silky, flat-lying hair (which doesn't mat) in all the Siamese range of point colors, possessing all the grace and elegance of Balinese dancers, the Balis are lively, affectionate and will work out in the garden with the family rather than be alone. Balis "talk." Not fussy eaters—it must be all the hunting they do in the garden.

Birmans
Sacred cat of Burma, with Siamese coat pattern, white gloved paws and semi-Persian coat. Its silky fur does not mat, but grooming is needed. Mixes well with other cats and children; loves playing.

Chinchilla
The "glamourpuss" with the turned-down mouth and white,

sometimes cream, undercoat, and grey, black or silver tipping. Affectionate and with a more docile nature than Persians. Grooming is needed for that silky coat.

Colorpoint Siamese

Persian long-hair and Siamese pattern, long graceful bodies, blue eyes and basic Siamese colors. Cuddly. Bossy. Demanding.

Himalayan
Another Persian–Siamese cross, the Himalayan has a chunky body with the Persian's long fur and the color points of the Siamese. Placid and affectionate. Grooming and bathing are necessary. They eat well and prefer a varied diet.

Persian
Still a showpony. Majestic, aloof, with squashed-in faces and constant grooming needed for that fluffy coat, which mats in an instant. Despite their short legs, Persians are active cats that enjoy getting down and dirty in the garden. Love playing, dislike the daily grooming. Can be fussy eaters if allowed.

Maine Coon
One of the biggest cats in the world, which can still boast being a good mouser. Evolved from working cats in Maine, at first glance it resembles a raccoon (hence the name), with its long flowing tabby coat and bushy tail. The Maines come in all colors, have a quiet "chirping" voice and enjoy human companionship. The long rough coat is medium to heavy and requires minimal grooming once a week. Despite their build and class, Maine Coons eat whatever ordinary working cats are eating.

Ragdolls
The Next Big Thing in the cat world. One of the larger domestic breeds, ragdolls have that limp, draped ragdoll like quality and make the most affectionate pets. Their coats are soft, medium to long, and require regular grooming (especially when in full molt). Placid and lovable "purr machines," they are at home in a house or an apartment that is stress-free. Big cats, big eaters.

Tortoiseshell
Patchwork coats of black and ginger, torties are always female (carrying a single ginger gene) with lovely natures in both domestic and pedigreed, short-haired and long-haired.

Turkish Van
The original swimming cat. From the Lake Van area in Turkey, exotic Vans enjoy swimming and playing in water. Distinctive cats with long silky hair, they make charming and very affectionate "personality" pets. Heavy

molters and shedders—grooming necessary. From simple origins, they eat a lot but don't demand gourmet food.

Short-hairs with attitude

Abyssinian

Lively, loyal, athletic and with quiet voices, Abys have patterned coats in shades from tawny to exotic. Easy to groom. They reach their paws around your neck and rub their heads under your chin in a most engaging way. Like access to a garden. Not fussy eaters; cheap to keep.

Burmese

A real family cat, affectionate and enjoys people, wanting to join in family activities. Burmese look like shorter, chunkier Siamese, but darker, with yellow eyes, and are complete extroverts, less chatty, not highly strung, and alert to "stranger danger." Easy to feed, if not spoiled. Like fresh grass.

British shorthair

A naturally stocky cat from solid, pedigreed British stock. They are often confused with common working-class mousers, the uninitiated not recognizing the finer points of breeding and the distinctive broad faces with round glowing, owl-like yellow eyes. Like blue bloods, they enjoy fresh meat, chicken or rabbit and probably would like an occasional piece of good British cheddar and a small side salad of green grass tips.

Cornish rex

Small cat, with an unusual wavy coat and a rather pointy head and big pointy ears. Lots of personality, clownish; a tail wagger and a loving companion. Both Cornish and Devon rexes feel the cold, with their short coats.

Devon rex

Dainty, with large ears and a pixie face, the rexie sports curly lashes, eyebrows and whiskers and a coat that is easily groomed. Chirrupy voice. Rexies like to know everything. They are big eaters, enjoy their food; good ground beef, a little egg yolk and cheese pleases.

Korat

From Thailand, these rare little cats, also called Si-Sawat (good fortune), have a blue sheen to their elegant coat, and green eyes. Too gentle to live amid the sudden or loud noises of larger households. A one-person cat, ideal for gentle owners working from home.

Manx

There are "rumpy," "stumpy," and "longie"—terms of endearment for the three bottoms-up types of tail-less Manx, who come from the Isle of Man. They have a distinctive hollow where their tail is supposed to be, looking like a cross between a rabbit and cat. Double coated, with a short, thick undercoat and a soft, medium-length top coat.

Oriental shorthair

Siamese with tabby or tortoiseshell-marked coats in a wide range of colors; green eyes. Lively and energetic, easily bored, need exercise and human companionship. They will be devoted pets as long as they are the boss. Good in apartments. Not fussy eaters, as long as there is best ground beef.

Scottish fold

Little Scottish cats with fold-over ears, bred in a wide range of colors and coat patterns, short-haired and long-haired. Gentle, friendly natures and well-padded bodies; can eat a lot.

Siamese

A challenging cat. Inquisitive chatterboxes with loud (very loud), carrying, demanding voices. Need constant attention. Bored Siams can be very destructive. Lonely Siams get depressed. But, ah, those brilliant blue eyes, those thoroughbred long legs, that whippy tail, the hues of those color points — and they won't break the housekeeping budget, foodwise.

Russian Blues

Sweet natured, affectionate and prefer an idle life indoors, like most blue bloods. Hearty Russian appetites, eating red meat, game, chicken, rice and grated vegetables, treats, cheese—anything you put in front of them (probably caviar and vodka too, if offered) to fill that chunky, solid frame. Chatters to their owners for food, and will hog the fire in winter. Big green eyes. Very companionable.

Somali

The long-haired Abyssinian with the plumed tail. A pretty cat that is fun-loving, affectionate and less boisterous than the Aby. Easy to groom. Not fussy about food.

Spotted mist

Cross between Burmese and the Abyssinian. The spotted mist looks like a lovely plump tabby with darker spots on a lighter misted background. They like fresh stewing meat certainly. An unpretentious cat.

Domestic short-hairs, working-class cats

Everyday cats, mouse-catchers, come in all shapes and sizes. Unlike dogs, there is little danger of a tiny kitten growing up into a 60 lb (30 kg) frame. Usually they are free, given away to a good home. Sometimes they just arrive at the back door or boldly push through the cat flap looking for food. If they find it, they stay.

Some will be closely connected to pedigreed breeds, with long shaggy coats or oriental markings but "without papers," as it is politely put. There are accidents in the best of families. Most domestics will be tabby, white or black.

Not all will be natural-born mousers or ratters, their traditional barnyard role. They will, if not discouraged, keep the birds from the garden. They will sometimes kill small animals, reptiles and rodents if they are at large.

Garden rules

for sensitive suburban cats

All cats should be "belled," with three or four good loud bells firmly attached to their collars, to keep them from catching birds. Most cats are cunning enough to slump their shoulders forward to muffle the bells in their furry chests if they forget themselves for a moment and stalk birds. "Bird lovers" in environmentally-conscious suburbs do not take kindly to seeing a cat streaking across their garden with a squawking bird in its mouth. (Neighbors used to regularly arrive to complain at our home because we had three black cats, always unjustly blamed.)

Cats should be kept indoors at night to protect the nocturnal wild animals and birds. Cats are natural night hunters if allowed out. They can climb trees to catch sleeping birds unawares or they can drag home more harmless game such as mice and rats, which they invariably let go and chase in the house in a traditional "torture" session. Inevitably, the mouse or rat flees behind a bookshelf or sofa until the cat, tiring of the game, loses interest and wanders off for a snack and a wash. It is left to the homeowner to find and catch the frightened prey.

I once pried a furious fruit bat away from a younger and slimmer cat called Golly Gosh, wrapped it in a towel one-handed while it dug claws and teeth into my other arm. It was 1 a.m. and the only way to get it back to the trees was to walk down the road in my nightgown. You have never seen a bat go as fast as that one after such a nocturnal adventure.

Care must be taken in the garden, too, to tie slippery cat-proof tin around tree trunks beneath feeding platforms and nesting sites for birds. Birdbaths should be carefully placed near thorny shrubs or cat-proof trees to be safer for the birds. Don't feed birds on the ground and pick up any spilt seeds from the ground to keep birds up out of cats' reach.

Releasing unwanted cats (and dogs) in the wild is also devastating to the animal wild-life. If the abandoned cat survives, it will kill a multitude of wild animals and birds to sustain itself, and may breed, producing more feral predators.

Name-a-cat

In *Old Possum's Book of Practical Cats*, T. S. Eliot said that every cat should have three names: one for its owner, such as "Peter, Augustus, Alonzo or James," one for feline friends, such as "Munkustrap, Quaxo, Coricopat, Bombalurina or Jellyorum," and one kept to itself.

There are literary cats: Eliot's Jennyanydots, Old Deuteronomy and Macavity. Lewis Carroll's Cheshire Cat and Holly Golightly's Cat in *Breakfast at Tiffany's* (Truman Capote). Beatrix Potter wrote about a cat called Simkins, belonging to the Tailor of Gloucester, who kept mice under upturned cups.

Famous people's famous cats: Florence Nightingale owned Bismark, Disraeli and Gladstone. Blatherskit, Buffalo Bill and Beelzebub belonged to Mark Twain.

Pattipaws was T. S. Eliot's real cat. The Clintons have a White House home page on the Internet for their cat Socks. Matthew Flinders' cat Trim went with him on the epic exploration around Australia.

Clean-a-cat

Dental care: All cats are susceptible to dental problems, bad breath, trouble eating, and excessive dribbling. Teeth cleaning, scaling and polishing (under anesthetic) may be avoided if the cat is fed raw chicken wings and hard dried food. Cat toothbrushes are also available.

Hairstyles: Double-sided brushes and steel combs will keep fur groomed. Mitts, even an attachment on the vacuum cleaner, will remove dead fur.

Bedding: Carpet deodorizers (also useful for floors and sofas) are available, but for cat hairs on furniture, try throw rugs, a strong vacuum cleaner and a damp chamois. Try the new washable beds if cats can be told where to sleep. They usually please themselves.

Litter box: Keep it in the laundry. Needs deep sides, deodorizer and one of the better quality litters.

Food bowls: Cats are very particular about their food bowls and may refuse to eat from a food bowl that is not kept clean. Fresh clean water should always be provided.

Carrying cats: Boxes or cages make life easier if you take the cat in the car. Plastic-based ones with sturdy wire tops can be lined with newspaper or old towels that can be thrown away. If the cat yowls loudly, it might be happier under a light cloth where it can't see the expressway traffic.

Feeding cats

Bringing up cats

Hand-rearing a tiny, abandoned kitten is very rewarding, but it should only be considered if there is no alternative available (do you know of any cat with kittens in the neighborhood, which might "foster"?)—and if you have a lot of time. Only take home a stray when you are quite sure it has been orphaned. If the mother is still seen in the neighborhood, she may be continuing to care for her offspring.

Can you take care of the kitten? It will need feeding every six to eight hours, including during the night. Are you home all day or can you take it with you to work? Can you make up special formulas? Will it be safe from other pets in the home? You must make a commitment for as long as it takes to hand-rear and, pay veterinary costs, then either keep it or find it a good home.

The first step is to keep it warm and quiet. Line a small box with natural materials like cotton and wool (an old woollen beanie makes a fine cocoon). Kittens do little more than sleep and eat in their first weeks.

Orphan kittens should be fed a formula close to a normal queen's milk, which is very high in protein (about twice as much as cow's milk, five times more than human breastmilk) and high in fat. Commercially-prepared formulas are available from vets for feeding orphaned kittens, or a formula can be easily made up at home.

Formula for kittens

Blend 1 egg yolk, 1 teaspoon cod-liver oil, 1 drop infant multi-vitamins, 1/2 cup of whole or evaporated milk.

Age weeks	Daily dosage to 3 1/2 oz/100g body weight
1	2 1/2 teaspoons
2	3 1/2 teaspoons
3	4 teaspoons
4	4 1/2 teaspoons

The amount of formula the kitten receives is related to its body weight. For instance, a

4 ounce/125 gram kitten needs 47.5 calories a day for its first week, a little more than three teaspoons over 24 hours. If this is too much per feed for the kitten in three feeds, feeds must be increased to six-hourly feeds. At every feed the kitten should eat until it is just nicely full—never until the stomach is tight and distended. Kittens overfed milk can develop diarrhea; it is better to underfeed for the first few days for this reason.

All of the feeding equipment must be kept scrupulously clean, and the formula must be given at body temperature. Feed the kitten from an eye-dropper or a toy baby's bottle. Commercial bottles and tiny feeding teats are available from vets.

To feed the kitten, hold it on its tummy, gently open the lips and slip the smallest sized nipple, with a few drops of the formula oozing through, into the kitten's mouth. Once it has tasted the milk and if it is hungry, it will begin to suck vigorously.

It should gain 2–4 ounces/50–100 grams a week. By the end of the third week, it should be weaned onto mashed/liquid food and begin lapping milk from a small saucer.

After every feed, moisten a cotton swab or tissue with warm water and gently wipe the orphan kitten's genital area to stimulate urination and defecation (something the mother cat usually takes care of).

By four or five weeks, when the kitten has been weaned, it is time to develop good eating habits. The kitten will begin by lapping milk and eating a little meat or fish if it is finely ground or chopped.

Baby foods can be tried. Kittens like the taste of creamed chicken and brains with vegetables. Chopped hard-boiled egg, soft-grated cheese and soft cooked, white chicken and grilled fish can be introduced, with raw ground beef.

Rickets aren't seen as much today because not many kittens eat only fresh meat. While calcium for strong bones is necessary, kittens don't like the taste of calcium powder mixed with their food, but it can be given in tablet or syrup form.

By 7 to 10 weeks, a weaned kitten can be separated from its mother. It should weigh 1–2 pounds/600–980 grams, be very active and spend its waking time at play.

Grown-up cats

The way to a cat's heart is definitely through its stomach. All cats—pedigrees and domestics—march on their stomachs. Cats will wake their owners at 5 a.m. for food if their bowls are empty. They need to know they are appreciated.

Cats need a high level of easily digestible

animal protein, together with animal fat and small quantities of essential vitamins and minerals. The diet must be based on animal tissue—meat, fish, chicken, liver, heart, kidneys. Cats appreciate novelty in food and by varying the diet you are less likely to have essential nutrient deficiencies.

Processed food

Canned foods: What you pay for is what you get. The cheaper brands of meat or fish contain more cereal bulk, in the form of soya bean protein (almost useless for carnivorous cats). Any can labeled "flavored" usually means it is an artificial taste, not containing real meat or fish.

Semi-moist foods: These contain meat, cereal, fats, added vitamins, chemicals (to give an attractive color) and preservatives.

Dry food: Usually contain cereals, some of the cheaper brands may not be well balanced. Cats adore the meat, chicken, fish and liver flavors. Some become quite addicted. Male cats should never eat dry food exclusively as this can lead to urinary problems. Bowls of fresh water should always be available.

The Cats' Pantry

Meat: Raw meat which contains fat is best for cats. They will eat ground meat, including liver and kidney, or baked and steamed meat that has retained its juices. A beaten egg yolk stirred through ground meat makes it more appealing if cats are being fussy.

Chicken: Cats enjoy raw chicken (score the skin), including whole wings and drumsticks, grilled chicken, boiled chicken, and baked chicken, minus bones.

Fish: Any kind of fish can be fed to cats, but the darker, oily fish (sprats, pilchards, herrings, sardines and so on) are the best, with tuna, which has the right amount of fat for the cat's diet. (Our cats are partial to small fish called silver biddies, which they eat scales, bones, small fins and all). They crunch up fleshier fish. Small sardines, shrimps or fish heads will be eaten by cats. Canned salmon and tuna and sardines in oil also add essential fatty acids.

Rabbit: The first fresh meat our cat Golly Gosh ate as an eight-week-old kitten was a rabbit as big as his mother, which she dragged home one very hot day. He never lost the taste for rabbit when he moved to the city, and preferred it raw (minus fur) from the butcher, cut up into rough joints, which he dragged all over the kitchen floor.

Eggs: Don't give cats egg whites, they find them hard to digest, but yolks are full of goodness.

Milk: Most cats love milk but some cats have difficulty digesting it because of a lactose intolerance. It is a good source of calcium, vitamin A and fat.

Cheese: A little grated cheddar will put calcium into the diets of Siamese, Burmese and those breeds that can't digest milk.

Water: Fresh water, changed daily, must be available for cats to digest their food properly.

Treats: Most cats will look for table scraps: titbits of a cooked chicken, including skin, meat and fatty bits; bacon rind and scraps of cooked meat and fish. Iodized salt in the cooking is important in the cats' diets and they enjoy gravy.

Vitamins and minerals: Cats require four vitamins and two minerals: vitamin A to stimulate growth, from cod-liver oil, egg yolk, ox liver and wheatflakes; vitamin D to absorb calcium and phosphate for bones, from cod liver oil and sunlight; vitamin E from red meat and wheat germ; and vitamin K from green vegetables and liver. Calcium and phosphates are needed to build bones, for blood and tissues and to aid in the absorption of nutrients; these minerals are found in red meat, milk and most foods.

Taurine: This is something that is worrying vets around the world who are treating increasing numbers of cats with eyesight problems. Taurine, an essential amino acid for cats (but not dogs), prevents damage to the retina, the light-sensitive membrane in the back of the eye. Some of the cheaper cat foods have been found to contain less than 0.05 per cent of taurine, deficiency of which leads to retinal degeneration and blindness in cats. Taurine is destroyed by heat but along with thiamine it is added to good quality commercial cat foods. For this reason "cat" tuna is better for your cat than "people" tuna. Taurine is contained in liver, kidney and milk. Cats must eat the foods containing taurine raw.

Grasses and plants: Cats love eating plain grass, which provides folic acid, one of the vitamins of the B-complex group. If cats are confined indoors, they should have small pots of lawn grasses and cocksfoot to help themselves to. Cats that rush outside to eat grass, then vomit, may be suffering from fur balls or worms.

There is also another little treat which will send cats wild – *Nepeta cataria*, a white-flowering catnip irresistible to every red-blooded cat. It is hard to keep in the garden because cats keep chewing it back to bare stalks, then rolling all over it. (It's used to stuff cat toys.) There is also another lemon-scented catnip (which can be used to take tea). Cats usually ignore the blue-flowering nepeta, a beloved cottage-garden flower.

"Beth had old-fashioned, fragrant flowers in her garden-sweet peas and mignonette, lark-spurs, pinks, pansies and southernwood, with chickweed for the bird and catnip for the pussies." Louisa M. Alcott's *Little Women*

F i n i c k y   e a t e r s

Cats often can be very particular about their food. It can be as simple as snacking or even stealing food from neighbors. Or a sudden dislike of the home menus can also occur.

Cats are highly sensitive to the slightest alteration in canned food recipes, sending desperate owners scouring supermarkets in unfamiliar suburbs for stock of a discontinued favorite brand. They will often eat only one label of a basic food. Owners sometimes open up to ten different brands before the cat will eat.

A simpler reason for the cat refusing to eat may be an unwashed food bowl, or stale food in the dish.

Your cat may prefer to eat only dried food for a while, then quite suddenly switch back to ground meat. It may refuse bought ground beef but eat steak chopped at home. If allowed, the cat can become addicted to liver or fish.

Loss of appetite may have more sinister causes, particularly if the cat appears unwell or skinny, and prompt professional advice should be sought.

Sick cats

Administering pills to cats is not easy. Cats hate medicine. Lay a large bath towel on a table, quickly lift up the cat—lay it across one end of the towel and—before it realizes what is happening—roll it up into a long, firm sausage shape, with the top of the towel snug under its outraged chin, to prevent it reaching out two furious paws to claw the hand attempting to administer the pill.

Have someone else hold the cat 'parcel' while you stand behind, holding the cat's head with one hand and lifting it, so that its bottom jaw falls open.

Hold the pill between the thumb and index finger of your other hand. With your index finger, push the pill at lightning speed into the cat's throat as far as possible before it can swing its head around or spit it out. Gently rub its throat to make it swallow the pill.

Liquid medicine can also be given using a plastic syringe, slid into the side of the cat's mouth and slowly squeezed.

Liquids-only diet

When a cat has a sore throat or cat virus and loses its sense of smell, it won't eat. For a liquid diet, blend half a 7 ounce/220 gram can of special cat food available from the vet with 5 fluid ounces/160 ml water and strain through a fine mesh. Use an eye dropper or syringe to squirt the food into the back of the cat's mouth a little at a time. This should give the cat normal fluid and nutrient needs. Excessive fluid losses (vomiting) must be replaced with added water.

Soft diet invalid foods

Good foods for the convalescent cat are strained baby foods. Strained egg yolk, with its high calories and easy digestibility, is good. Strained chicken, turkey, lamb or beef baby foods can also have egg yolks added; feed an adult cat 2 small jars but no more than 1 to 2 tablespoons per 4 pounds/2 kilograms body weight at each feed, to avoid vomiting. Sick cats should be given water by eye dropper if they show signs of dehydration. Chicken or beef broth can be used to thin blended foods to feed by hand and help meet the cat's fluid requirements.

Soft-boil eggs before giving them to the cat or mixing them in with other strained foods.

Restricted mineral and sodium diet

1 lb/500g cooked ground beef
4 oz/125g liver
1 cup cooked rice (no salt)
1 teaspoon vegetable oil
1 teaspoon calcium carbonate

Cook the meat and liver in the oil over a low heat. Add the rice and calcium. This a balanced veterinary diet which fulfills all the vitamin and trace-mineral needs.

Cats' allergy diets

Avoid suspected ingredients, especially protein sources such as meat that the cat may have been eating. If eating canned food, substitute a blander variety of chicken, lamb or plain fish.

If the skin or gastrointestinal allergy symptoms continue, allow the cat a test diet of only fresh steamed fish, white rice then chicken for up to two weeks. Avoid milk and any processed food.

If improvements are noted, potential allergens may be introduced singly into the cat's diet, allowing several days for symptoms to reappear. Once the allergen is identified, it is essential to permanently exclude it from the cat's diet because only small quantities are necessary to trigger a response.

Many pet foods contain several sources of protein, making identification of offending allergens difficult. Prescription ranges from vets are complete diets (in the canned form, using lamb and rice protein), which provide long-time care of food intolerance.

HG's kidney kebabs

Not only orientals will appreciate the eastern flavor of kebabs

INGREDIENTS
1 lamb kidney
1 or 2 shrimp
1 tablespoon oil
chopped catnip

METHOD
Skin and slice the kidney and quarter it.
Shell and slice the shrimp. Thread the pieces
of meat and seafood on a skewer and brush with oil.
Grill until just cooked, remove from skewer
and sprinkle with finely chopped catnip.

HG, a big black cat
who likes his food, favors this dish above all
others. The firm texture of the shrimp contrasts
with the creaminess of the kidney, only topped
by the crunchiness of the catnip.

Major-Major's chickenburgers

INGREDIENTS

2 $\frac{1}{2}$ oz/75g chicken flesh, ground or finely chopped
2 tablespoons fine fresh breadcrumbs or oatmeal
1 small egg yolk
dash of soy sauce

METHOD

Put all ingredients in a bowl and knead well.
Make tiny burgers and fry in a pan with a
few drops of oil, turning until lightly golden.
Remove from heat and cool,
then cut into cat-bite-sized pieces.

Roy's Sossypot fish platter

INGREDIENTS

3 ½ oz/100g frozen white fish filets

3 tablespoons brown breadcrumbs or breakfast cereal

1 small egg yolk

1 tablespoon oil

METHOD

Defrost the fish and cut into teaspoon-sized pieces. Coat with beaten egg and roll in breadcrumbs. Fry in oil until golden brown. Drain and cool, then serve with some chopped catnip. (Roy prefers cereal softened with egg yolk, though he usually eats his fish raw.)

Microwave fish

METHOD

Use frozen or fresh fileted fish and cook for 2 or 3 minutes until the flesh is white in the microwave. Remove the fish and carefully remove any bones. Mash the flesh with a fork.

Steak tartare

METHOD

Finely chop a steak. Beat 1 egg yolk and stir into the steak.
Form into loose balls about the size of a teaspoon and serve.

Aunty Jack mince

Helen Rook, a rural nurse, has six cats, rescued from floods, grass fires, industrial garbage bins, drains or who just conveniently turned up near her remote property. Once a week, she makes up a big pot of gourmet mince which meets with their unanimous approval. The cats, Mandy, Poppy (she pops in and out), Powder Puff, Snowflake (black kitten found in a big garbage bin but turned out to be white after a bath), Ginger Meggs and Maggie (black and white like the pet magpie) would rip your hands off to get another serve of this mince.

INGREDIENTS

4 lb/2 kg ground beef
1 onion, chopped
1 garlic clove, chopped
1 teaspoon iodized salt
1 dessertspoon wheatgerm
2 cups brown or white rice

METHOD

Put all the ingredients in a large pot with a little water (some moisture will come out of the meat). More water can be added if it is needed. Cook for about 10 to 20 minutes (until the rice is cooked), then remove from the heat and cool. Drain off the juice (which can be used with wheatgerm and dried cat food) and divide into daily portions to keep in the refrigerator or freezer.

Note: Since Powder Puff (found at the edge of a flooded stream with two other starving kittens) had a broken jaw, Helen has fed her with just lightly grilled chicken wings to keep her back teeth in good condition. Boiled chicken and rice is another favorite of the Rook cats, which adore fatty bits cut from stewing meat.

Mister Mistoffelees grilled fish

INGREDIENTS
2 filets of fish
margarine
1 teaspoon lemon juice

METHOD
Wipe filets with a kitchen towel and place on a grill tray with lemon juice on foil and dab with margarine. Grill until golden brown then turn over, using more margarine, until skin browns and bubbles—don't overcook the fish flesh. Cut up the fish and serve.

Note: Mister loved this grilled fish even more than fresh fish from the fish markets. It was enough to tempt his appetite after a bad attack of cat flu and croup, when an electric frying pan of water had to be used all night to make steam to keep him breathing.

Susie Wong's Chinese chicken

INGREDIENTS

$^1/_2$ chicken breast or 2 chicken thighs
dash of soy sauce
3 tablespoons water
2 tablespoons oil
1 cup cooked rice
garnish of tiny dried Chinese shrimps
zucchini

METHOD

Cut the chicken into tiny slivers and fry in the oil until just cooked. Mix the soy sauce in the water, add to pan and stir in the cooked rice. Strips of cooked chicken skin can be added with the shrimps as a garnish. If the cat likes cooked vegetables, slivers of zucchini can be added.

Pearl and Vicky's green salad

METHOD

Pull handfuls of fresh sweet grass from the garden and finely chop Nepeta (catnip) and toss. Finely chopped celery could be added to the green salad. Note: Vicky eats a lot of dried food and loves salad. Mr Mistoffelees used to attack the shopping bags, looking for the fresh green celery leaves. If some leaves and bits of stalk were put with his food, he would always chew the celery first.

Ginger Meggs' killer snacks

Meggs was completely addicted to dried biscuits, often rattling his paw around the box on top of the refrigerator in the middle of the night. For medical reasons, he was no longer able to eat dried food and it had to be suddenly withdrawn but, like many addicts, he could not go "cold turkey." This recipe is our solution.

METHOD

Add to 1 tablespoon of dry cat food, margarine or oil from a sardine can and other flavors are introduced—chopped liver or kidney, flakes of canned fish, gravy or a strong chicken stock. This can be reduced to 1 1/2, then 1 teaspoon of a veterinary-approved brand of dry food until the cat is gradually weaned off the dry food.

Puddy's puddin diet

At one stage a slim tabby cat called Uhu, for her owl-like eyes, became Puddy due to weight gain from a hormone imbalance. Besides pills, Puddy went on a strict slimming diet. This was one of her meals. Amounts can be doubled to cook a larger amount.

INGREDIENTS
$^1/_3$ cup long-grain white rice
$^2/_3$ cup lean meat
1 oz/30g liver
3 teaspoons bonemeal
1 teaspoon corn oil
$^1/_2$ teaspoon iodized salt
1 $^1/_2$ cups water

METHOD
Cook the rice, salt, oil and bonemeal in the water. Cover and simmer for 10 minutes once boiling. Add meat and liver and cook for several minutes. Take off the heat and cool. This dish can be refrigerated for several days. Yields enough food to last an average cat three days. It provides 31% protein, 41% fat and 28% carbohydrate for cats. Fish or chicken can be substituted for meat if the cat prefers to eat them. The liver can also be chopped finely and mixed through the cooked food to tempt the cat. To cut the fat further, use safflower oil instead of corn oil.

Lucky Lucifer's low-fat liver

Don't overcook, or it loses the appetizing smell so attractive to cats.

INGREDIENTS

1 lb/500g liver cooked, then chopped finely in a processor
5 oz/175g white rice, cooked
1 teaspoon vegetable oil
1 teaspoon calcium carbonate

METHOD

Put the chopped liver in a dish with the rice, oil and calcium and stir well. Put out in small
portions until the slimmer becomes used to the new rations.

Fish and potato soup

INGREDIENTS
3 large potatoes, peeled
1 clove garlic, sliced
1 onion, peeled
1 carrot
2 tablespoons oil
1 cup water
1 cup milk
1 lb/500g fish, fresh or canned
1 cup cooked rice

METHOD
Cook the potatoes in boiling water until they are breaking up then
sieve or mash them. Grate the onion and carrot. Using a large pan,
lightly saute the garlic, onion and carrot in the oil. Add the
water and the milk, and simmer for a few minutes.
Put in the potatoes and fish (use fresh
boneless fish or cheap canned salmon)
and serve with cooked rice.

Lamb heart

INGREDIENTS
1 lamb heart
wholewheat flour
oil
mashed potato

METHOD

These hearts are quite small, and suitable for cats. Clean and cut into 1 inch/ 2.5 cm slices. Dip the slices into wholemeal flour (or breadcrumbs and beaten egg yolk) and fry in oil for about 5 minutes until brown on both sides. Cut the heart slices up and mix with mashed potatoes and the pan scrapings.

Jellied chicken

INGREDIENTS

1 lb/500g chicken wings
2 cloves of garlic, peeled
1 onion
1 stalk of celery
a handful of green beans
water

METHOD

This is the sort of food you can cook while you are busy doing something else.

Put the chicken wings into a pan and add enough water to cover. Coarsely chop the garlic, onion, celery and beans and add to the pan. Simmer for about 20-30 minutes. Remove the chicken wings and vegetables from the water and remove all the meat from the chicken bones. Dice the meat. Set the meat and vegetables aside and put the bones back into the pot of water. Simmer for about two hours to make a good stock. Discard the bones and return the reserved meat and vegetables to the stock. Refrigerate until set.

Sunday night suppers

INGREDIENTS
2 egg yolks
1 tablespoon milk
2 tablespoons oil
4 oz/125g ground beef
a handful of grated cheese
parsley

METHOD
Beat the eggs with the milk in a bowl until frothy. Put the oil in a pan and brown the beef in it. Add the egg mixture and the grated cheese. Cook slowly over a low heat, stirring. You can add a little parsley for taste.